AUTHENTIC BRAZILIAN

BOSSA NOV

GUITAR ARRANGEMENTS

Arranged by
JACK MARSHALL

CONTENTS

ISBN 978-0-7935-0514-2

HAL•LEONARD®
CORPORATION
7777 W. BLUEMOUND RD. P.O. BOX 13819 MILWAUKEE, WI 53213

Visit Hal Leonard Online at
www.halleonard.com

INTRODUCTION

In recent years the Bossa Nova has become much more than just a passing fancy on the American musical scene. The guitar is a very important part of the Bossa Nova style and the great Brazilian composers responsible for many of our "standards" are all guitarists: Antonio Carlos Jobim, Luiz Bonfa, Laurindo Almeida, Baden Powell and Joao Gilberto.

The basic rhythm pattern for guitar accompaniment is as follows:

But there are many variations in the Bossa Nova rhythm patterns, some of which are shown here:

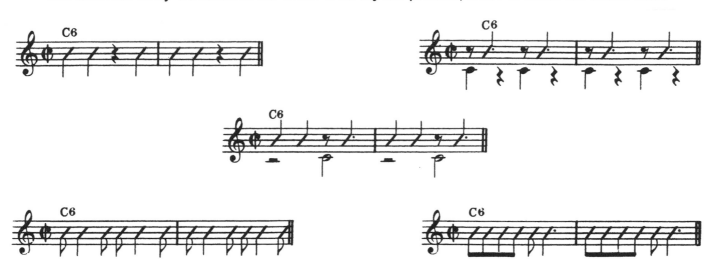

In the following rhythm pattern notice the first beat and chord change of each measure is anticipated:

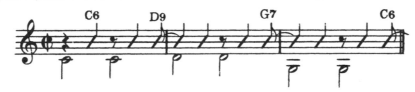

EXPLANATION OF FINGERINGS

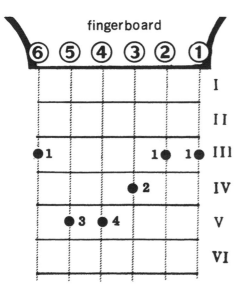

Encircled numbers ① — ⑥ indicate the string to be used.

Roman numerals indicate the fret position.

Arabic numerals (1, 2, 3, 4) indicate the proper left-hand fingering.

For example: The "G" chord in the third position (III) may look like this:

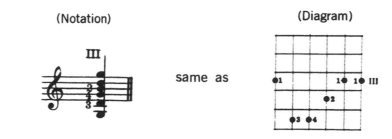

(Notation)   same as   (Diagram)

GARÔTA DE IPANEMA
(The Girl from Ipanema)

Music by ANTONIO CARLOS JOBIM
English Words by NORMAN GIMBEL
Original Words by VINICIUS DE MORAES

DEIXA
(Let Me)

Music by BADEN POWELL
English Lyrics by NORMAN GIMBEL

SAMBA DE UMA NOTA SO
(One Note Samba)

Original Lyrics by NEWTON MENDONCA
English Lyrics by ANTONIO CARLOS JOBIM
Music by ANTONIO CARLOS JOBIM

UM ABRACO NO BONFA

By JOAO GILBERTO

CORCOVADO
(Quiet Nights of Quiet Stars)

English Words by GENE LEES
Original Words and Music by ANTONIO CARLOS JOBIM

SAMBALERO

By LUIZ BONFA

THESE ARE THE WAYS OF LOVE

Words and Music by JACK MARSHALL
and BOB MOSHER

DESTINO

Words and Music by
LAURINDO ALMEIDA

HO-BA-LA-LA

Words and Music by NORMAN GIMBEL
and JOAO GILBERTO

O BARQUINHO
(Little Boat)

Original Lyric by RONALDO BOSCOLI
English Lyric by BUDDY KAYE
Music by ROBERTO MENESCAL

INSENSATEZ
(How Insensitive)

Music by ANTONIO CARLOS JOBIM
Original Words by VINICIUS DE MORAES
English Words by NORMAN GIMBEL

MEDITACÁO
(Meditation)

Music by ANTONIO CARLOS JOBIM
Original Words by NEWTON MENDONÇA
English Words by NORMAN GIMBEL

BIM-BOM

Words and Music by
JOAO GILBERTO

HERE LIES LOVE

Words and Music by JACK MARSHALL
and BOB MOSHER

JOURNEY TO RECIFE

By RICHARD EVANS
and NORMAN GIMBEL

LUCIANA

Words by VINICIUS DE MORAES
Music by ANTONIO CARLOS JOBIM

Moderately slow

REZA

By EDU LOBO
and RUY GUERRA

SÓZINHA NÃO

By CHICO

TRISTEZA EM MIM

By JOSE GUIMARAES
and MAURO TAVARES

MENINA FLOR

Words by MARIA TOLEDO
Music by LUIZ BONFA